やるべきですよ。 You should do it.
やらなきゃいけない。 You must do it.
君はやったの？ Did you do it?

やる　　　やった　　やっちゃった
do it　　did it　　have done it
do it　　did it　　have done it

やったね！！ We made it!

Written by Mikiko Nakamoto / Narration : Dario Toda　　Music : Shinya Morimoto　　©2017

CONTENTS

unit		topics	page
1	1	Me Myself　大地の自己紹介	4
	2	The Beautiful Planet　美しい惑星ー地球ー	6
	3	The Mayor's Speech　市長演説	8
2	1	Hello. Come in. Help yourself.　お友達の家へ	10
	2	Surprising Facts　おどろくべき動物たち	12
	3	My Past, Present and Future　ぼくの過去・現在・未来	14
3	1	Recycling Garbage　リサイクルを考える	16
	2	Starting off on a World Trip　世界旅行プラン	18
	3	Asking Permission　もう、十分な年齢です	20
4	1	My Routine Activities　ぼくと妹の日課	22
	2	I did not do anything bad.　ぼくの言い分	24
	3	I failed the test.　テストに落ちた理由	26
5	1	A Post Card from Hawaii　ハワイからの絵葉書	28
	2	I was the smallest tree in the forest.　セコイアの木	30
	3	STORY: The Cow and the Frog　イソップ物語　牛とカエル	32
6	1	I want to stop by a convenience store to buy something to drink.　コンビニに寄りたい	34
	2	I want you to leave me along.　僕のことはかまわないで	36
	3	I told you to do this.　言ったでしょ	38
7	1	Offering Good Advice　アドバイスしてみよう	40
	2	I wish I could.　できたら良いのに	42
	3	Show and Tell　お気に入りのおもちゃ	44
8	1	The man wearing a bright pink sweater　どの人？	46
	2	A bird whose beak is yellow　くちばしが黄色い鳥	48
	3	STORY: The Peach Boy　桃太郎の簡単バージョンと詳しいバージョン	50
9	1	Have you seen it yet?　もう見た？	52
	2	Have you seen a snake with legs?　見たことある？	54
	3	The most beautiful sunset I have ever seen.　今までの中で一番！	56
10	1	Where have you been?　どこに行ってたの？	58
	2	STORY: Jack and the Beanstalk　ジャックと豆の木	60
	3	The language spoken there is English.　そこで話されている言語は英語です	62
supplement		Listening Test　Units 1-2	64
		Units 3-4	65
		Units 5-7	66
		Units 8-10	67
		Irregular verbs	68
		Grammar Points	70
		Words and Phrases Glossary	73
		Song: Occupation Song	76
		Song: 'Cause You're My Friend	77

Learning World 5 for TOMORROW

Mikiko Nakamoto

Ken

Claire

Daichi

Ibuki

Naomi

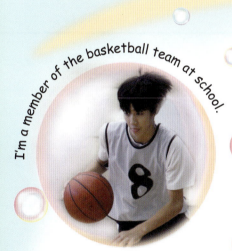
I'm a member of the basketball team at school!

Have you ever seen a pig, a pig with wings?

a bird whose beak is yellow

I want you to study hard.

These are the best pancakes I've ever had.

She became as big as a dog!

ラーニングワールドシリーズは全10巻から成り、幼児から中学生まで、それぞれの発達段階と学習年数に応じて書かれています。本シリーズはヒューマニスティック・アプローチとコミュニカティブ・アプローチを取り入れ、従来の暗記とパターンプラクティス中心の英語教育ではなく、「答え1つでない」英語による言語教育を目指しています。発話に重要な「自分の意見の構築」「自尊心の育成」「他者への許容」等が英語の4技能の学習を通して習得できるようにしています。本書はシリーズ9巻目で、Learning World for Tomorrow（初版1998年発行）の改訂版です。

全10ユニットのうち前半のユニットは既習の文構造を使ってより深く、より現実に即した英語を使えるように構成されています。後半のユニットでは助動詞、仮定法、関係代名詞、現在完了、受動態などの文構造をその「機能」を重視して扱い、文法問題を解けることを目的とするのではなく、ターゲットの文構造を使って**学習者の思考能力を高め、自分自身の答えを見つけ**、他の学習者との**ディスカッションを経て効果的なプレゼンテーション**をおこなえるように構成しています。

幼児・児童英語学習経験5年以上の小学生、中学生に効果的に使用することができます。

● このテキストには次のマークがページごとに示されています。●

Passage
意味を考えながら読みましょう。

Speech
自分で考えた英文を大きな声で発表しましょう。

Dialogue
登場人物になったつもりで会話を覚えましょう。

Reading
英文から内容を読みとりましょう。

Chant
リズムにのってまるごと覚えましょう。

Listening Test
英語をよく聞いて答えましょう。

Story
流れをつかみながらじっくり読みましょう。

Song
歌詞を覚えて歌いましょう。

Grammar Point
新しく習う構文を理解しましょう。

Chant for Grammar
リズムで動詞の変化や構文を丸ごと覚えましょう。

これだけできるようにがんばろう。

Achievement Targets

1. テキスト4-5ページを参考に15以上の文を使って自己紹介ができます。
Able to introduce myself using at least 15 sentences.

2. 8以上の文を使って自分の住んでいる町を紹介することができます。
Able to introduce the city I live in using at least 8 sentences.

3. 炊飯器を使ってご飯の炊き方を説明することができます。
Able to explain how to cook rice with a rice cooker.

4. 自分がいつもしている日課を5つ usually を使って説明できます。
Able to describe 5 things I do using “usually”.

5. 明日しようと決めていることを am going to を使って3つ言うことができます。
Able to say 3 things I have decided to do tomorrow using “am going to”.

6. 自分が知っている人物を１人決めて5文以上でプレゼンテーションができます。
Able to make a presentation on a person I know using at least 5 sentences.

7. 最近あまり眠れない友達に3つアドバイスができます。
Able to give 3 pieces of advice to my friend who can’t sleep well these days.

8. もし自分が今大学生だったら何をするかを3つ以上言うことができます。
Able to say 3 things I would do if I were a university student.

9. 友達に招待されましたが忙しくていけません。ていねいに断ることができます。
Able to decline my friend’s invitation because I am too busy.

10. 桃太郎ってだれ？とたずねられました。説明することができます。
Able to explain who Momotaro is.

11. テキストのスピーチのページから2つ選んでプレゼンテーションができます。
Able to make presentations on 2 ‘Speech’ topics. ⑨ ㉟ ㊲ ㊶ ㊺ (55) (57)

12. テキストの Reading のノンフィクションを１つ選んで暗記し発表することができます。
Able to recite 1 non-fiction story from the ‘Reading’ pages. ⑦ ㉓ ㉟ ㊼

13. テキストの中の を6つ以上暗唱できます。
Able to recite at least 6 chants from the ‘Chants’ section.
⑥ ⑩ ⑯ ㉔ ㊱ ㊳ ㊷ ㊽ (52) (54) (58) (62)

14. テキストの中の を4つ以上暗記して友達と一緒に言うことができます。
Able to remember and say at least 4 dialogues with a partner. ⑳ ㉖ ㉞ ㊵ ㊻ (56)

15. テキストの中の を2つ暗記して発表することができます。
Able to recite 2 stories from the ‘Story’ pages. ㉜ ㊿ (60)

16. テキストの中の を3つ以上暗記して発表することができます。
Able to recite at least 3 passages from the ‘Passage’ pages.
④ ⑥ ⑧ ⑫ ⑭ ⑱ ㉒ ㉘ ㉚ ㊹

○の中の数字はページをあらわしています。

Hello, everyone. Let me introduce myself.

My name is Asahi Daichi.

Daichi is my given name and Asahi is my family name.

In Japan, we usually say our family name first.

I have one little sister. Her name is Ibuki.

I am twelve years old. Ibuki is eight years old.

I go to Lake View Junior High School. I am in the seventh grade.

I am good at running. I can run fast.

I am a member of the basketball team at school.

I enjoy playing basketball with my friends after school.

I like math and science. I don't like music.

Ibuki can play the piano very well, but I can't.

My father is a music teacher. Of course, he can play the piano, too.

My mother is an office worker. She is good at singing.

1B

Unit 1

Me Myself

Check any words which fit you.

1 I am good at
- ☐ sports ( )
- ☐ math
- ☐ science
- ☐ singing
- ☐ playing a musical instrument ( )
- ☐ making friends
- ☐ _____
- ☐ _____

2 I am afraid of
- ☐ snakes
- ☐ spiders
- ☐ traveling in airplanes
- ☐ being alone
- ☐ blood
- ☐ heights
- ☐ big dogs
- ☐ thunderstorms
- ☐ speaking in front of people
- ☐ _____
- ☐ _____

3 I enjoy
- ☐ playing with my friends
- ☐ studying at school
- ☐ helping my mother
- ☐ playing ( )
- ☐ watching TV
- ☐ reading books
- ☐ gardening
- ☐ talking with my friends
- ☐ traveling
- ☐ _____
- ☐ _____

4 I like
- ☐ meeting new people
- ☐ being on my own
- ☐ playing team sports
- ☐ doing the ironing
- ☐ camping
- ☐ eating out
- ☐ _____
- ☐ _____

5 I am
- ☐ a good student
- ☐ very organized
- ☐ a good cook
- ☐ a good listener
- ☐ intelligent
- ☐ _____
- ☐ _____

In the future,

6 I want
- ☐ to study at university
- ☐ to be rich
- ☐ to live abroad
- ☐ to have a big family
- ☐ to be famous
- ☐ _____
- ☐ _____

5
five

Unit 1 2A

5→6

Round and round,
The earth goes around.
Spring, summer, fall and winter.
Round and round,
The earth goes around.

Round and round,
The earth spins around.
Morning, afternoon, evening and night.
Round and round,
The earth spins around.

7→8

What are you doing?
I'm getting up.
I'm studying at school.
I'm eating lunch.
I'm coming home.
I'm having dinner.
I'm taking a bath.
I'm going to bed.
Be quiet, please. I am sleeping.

2B

Identify the person

Exchange information and write the names of each person.

( )( )( )( )( )

( )( )( )( )

🎵 9

Reading

What causes night and day?

The earth spins on its axis as it travels around the sun. The side of the earth facing the sun gets light and heat. We call this daytime. The other side of the earth is cool and dark, which is night. Earth's axis is tilted, so this causes different seasons.

(①the sun ②axis ③spin ④heat
⑤light ⑥the earth ⑦go around the sun)

Hello, ladies and gentlemen:

I am the mayor of this city. My name is Asahi Daichi.

Please call me Mr. Mayor.

I'm kind, intelligent, brave and sincere.

Today, I am very happy to introduce our city to you.

The name of the city is Sunflower.

The population of our city is 354,325.

There are two kindergartens, two elementary schools,

and one high school in this city. There is a library, a bank,

a post office, a fire station, a police station, two big supermarkets,

a hospital and a train station.

We are proud of our beautiful park in front of the library.

You are welcome to visit us any time.

Thank you.

3B   Unit 1

Speech: Mayor's Speech

1 The name of our new city:

2 The population of our city:

3 What we need in our new city:

☐ restaurant   ☐ post office   ☐ police station   ☐ park   ☐ hospital   ☐ city hall
☐ music hall   ☐ train station   ☐ elementary school   ☐ high school   ☐ fire station
☐ supermarket   ☐ convenience store   ☐ amusement park   ☐ bakery   ☐ department store

☐ _____   ☐ _____   ☐ _____

4 The characteristics of a good mayor:

☐ friendly   ☐ kind   ☐ popular   ☐ cool   ☐ smart   ☐ shy   ☐ sincere   ☐ adventurous
☐ brave   ☐ athletic   ☐ tough   ☐ optimistic   ☐ energetic   ☐ young   ☐ diligent   ☐ cheerful
☐ honest   ☐ ambitious   ☐ intelligent   ☐ noisy   ☐ quiet   ☐ humorous   ☐ unique

☐ _____   ☐ _____   ☐ _____

My name is _____. Please call me _____.

I am the mayor of this city.

I am _____, _____, _____, and _____.

Today, I am very happy to introduce our city to you.

The name of our city is _____.

The population is _____.

There are _____

_____

_____ in our city.

We are proud of _____. Thank you.

Hello. How are you? Nice to see you again.

Come in. Have a seat. Make yourself at home.

Have some cookies. Help yourself. They are very good!

 I'm so happy to be here!

I'm glad to hear that.

Good-bye. It was fun. Hope to see you again.

Say hello to your family. Let's keep in touch.

Write me a letter. E-mail me. It will be fun!

1B Unit 2

How to use a Rice Cooker

Write the number to put the sentences in order so that you can cook rice with a rice cooker.

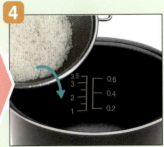

- [ ] Rinse the rice and drain the water several times.
- [ ] Put the rice into a bowl.
- [ ] Press the "Cook" button. The rice cooker will beep when the rice is done.
- [ ] Put the rice into the pot of the rice cooker.
- [ ] Add water using the scale on the inside of the pot.
- [ ] The rice cooker will automatically switch to the "Keep Warm" mode.
- [ ] Use a cup to measure the rice. (1 cup = 2 cups of cooked rice)

Various Greetings

A: Long time no see.
B: I'm so glad to see you.

A: How've you been?
B: Just fine.

A: Thank you.
B: It's my pleasure.

A: Have a happy new year.
B: Thank you. You too.

A: It was nice seeing you again.
B: It was nice seeing you, too.

A: Is this seat taken?
B: No, it's empty.

A: Hello. This is Ken.
B: Hi, Ken. Hold on a second. I'll get Cindy.

Unit 2 2A

Surprising Facts

Dolphins sleep with one eye open.

Butterflies taste with their feet.

Crows remember human faces for years.

Elephants have only four teeth.

Snails have more than 2,500 teeth.

Squids have three hearts.

Only male sea horses give birth.

Lions sleep fifteen hours a day.

Giraffes sleep twenty minutes a day.

Pandas eat meat.

Ostriches' eggs weigh 1,500 grams.

Writing a letter

Dear Mr. Dracula,
Hello, Mr. Dracula. My name is Ibuki.
I am eight years old.
I have some questions for you.
Do you often go to the dentist?
Why do you like blood?
What blood type do you like?
Can you eat hamburgers, too?
What time do you go to bed?
Please write me a letter.
I am waiting for your answers.
              Love always,
              Ibuki xo

Write a letter to someone you know.

Beethoven, Helen Keller, Natsume Soseki, Albert Einstein, Pablo Picasso, Walt Disney,
Harry Potter, Cinderella, Doraemon, Nobita, Snow White, Anpanman, Urashima Taro

A letter to

Dear _____ ,

Surprising Facts

Write three facts from the left page that surprised you the most.

1.
2.
3.

I was a little egg. I was sleeping on a leaf.

Now I am a caterpillar. I am eating leaves.

One day, I will be a butterfly, and I will fly in the sky.

I was a little egg. I was sleeping in the mud.

Now I am a tadpole. I am swimming in a pond.

One day, I will be a frog, and I will hop on the land.

I was a little baby. I was playing in my father's arms.

Now I am a boy. I am studying at school.

One day, I will be an astronaut, and I will go into space.

3B

Unit 2

Spot the differences

Tell the differences between the two pictures using "is/are" and "was/were".

Write three of the differences.

Ex. In picture 1, there was a ... on the table, but in Picture 2, there is ... on the TV.
In picture 1, the boy was ...ing, but in Picture 2, he is ...ing.

1
2
3

Story Writing

Write a story using "I was/ I am/ I will be". Draw pictures to go with the story.

I was

I am

I will be

Unit 3 1A

 What's the matter?

 Well... There is a problem. I don't know what to do with them.

What are we going to do with them?

      Cans and bottles, cans and bottles.

What are we going to do with them?

      Plastic bags and styrofoam trays.

Throw them away?   Use them again?

What are we going to do with them?

1B Unit 3

® The 3Rs: Reduce, Reuse, Recycle

Separate the waste into the correct bins.

1 Garbage: • Kitchen scraps, paper and yard trimmings

2 Recycling:
• Empty and flatten cardboard boxes
• Clean and rinse glass bottles and jars
• Clean and flatten plastic bottles

Cardboard bin:

Newspaper bin:

Glass & metal bin:

Plastic bin:

cardboard boxes	flyers	pizza boxes	shampoo bottles	junk mail
styrofoam trays	plastic bags	egg shells	dish soap bottles	
writing paper	potato skins	fish bones	plastic lids	newspapers
food containers	jam jars	fallen leaves	envelopes	beer cans

Check things you and your family do to reduce waste.

☐ Use cloth bags or reusable shopping bags instead of plastic bags at the store

☐ Buy food that has less packaging

☐ Don't buy bottled drinks, but use your own bottles

☐ Donate items when possible

☐ Follow your city's recycling policies

☐

 What do you want to do when you grow up?

 I want to travel around the world.
Let me tell you my plan!

I will go to Australia and climb Uluru with koalas and kangaroos.

Then I will go to India and swim in the Ganges River with an elephant.

Then I will go to Turkey and live in a cave with an ibex.

Then I will go to Algeria and ride on a camel in the Sahara Desert.

Then I will go to Italy and play soccer at the Colosseum.

Then I will go to Venezuela and see the Angel Falls.

Then I will come back home and have a good rest.

18
eighteen

Unit 3

Let's go around the world! – The funniest itinerary

Write nine different kinds of transportation

                                                                date and month   year

1 I will leave Japan on _____ in _____.

2 I will go to _____ by _____.

   It will take me _____ days to get to _____ by _____.

3 Then I will go to _____ by _____.

   It will take me _____ days to get to _____ by _____.

4 Then I will go to _____ by _____.

   It will take me _____ days to get to _____ by _____.

   I will have fun!

Based on your itinerary, draw lines from place to place to show your travel route.

 Dad, may I go to Hawaii to visit Uncle James?

 By yourself? Of course not.

 Why not?

 Because you are too young to go to Hawaii by yourself.

 No, I'm not! I'm not too young.

I am old enough to go there by myself.

I can do anything by myself.

 Can you get along well with your cousins?

 Of course I can. I can get along well with them.

 All right. Be sure to behave yourself.

 Thank you, Dad.

Unit 3

Check your accuracy

Try to do it without looking at a ruler or a watch. Measure to see how close you were.

1 Draw a 4 cm line.   too long   too short   just right

2 Draw a 10 cm line.   too long   too short   just right

3 Draw an 8.5 cm line.   too long   too short   just right

4 Stand up for 30 seconds and then sit down.   too long   too short   just right

The first student astronaut

1 Something I am good at:

2 Something I like doing:

3 My favorite subject:

You were selected to be the first student to travel to the moon.
あなたは、月へ行く最初の生徒として選ばれました。
どうして選ばれたのか考えてみましょう。

Why were you chosen for this trip?

I was chosen because

Unit 4 1A

I have a little sister. Her name is Ibuki. She is eight years old.

I usually get up at 6:00, but Ibuki gets up at 6:30.

I usually make my bed at 7:00, but Ibuki makes her bed at 7:30.

I usually have breakfast at 7:15, but Ibuki has breakfast at 8:00.

I usually go to school at 8:00, but Ibuki goes to school at 8:20.

I usually study English at 9:00, but Ibuki studies English at 9:15.

I usually do my homework at 4:30, but Ibuki does her homework at 3:45.

I usually take a bath at 8:00, but Ibuki takes a bath at 7:30.

I usually watch TV at 8:30, and Ibuki watches TV at 8:30, too.

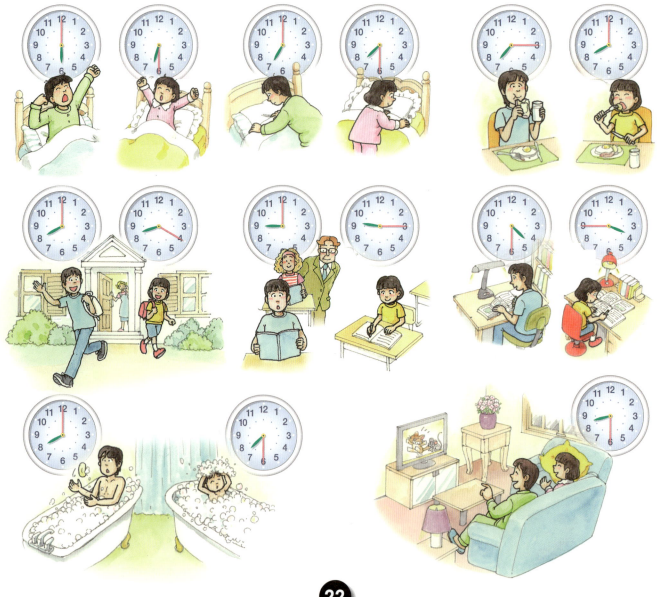

1B

Unit 4

28

have has	go goes	do does	run runs	come comes	read reads
fly flies	cry cries	study studies	walk walks	help helps	speak speaks
want wants	write writes	eat eats	use uses	lose loses	choose chooses
wash washes	catch catches	teach teaches			

People and Occupations

Write the names of each person, and his/her occupation.

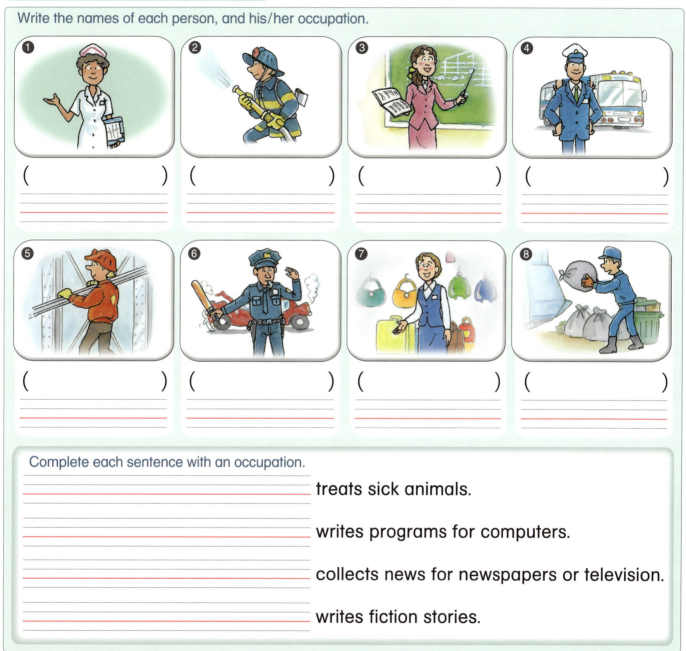

1. (   )
2. (   )
3. (   )
4. (   )
5. (   )
6. (   )
7. (   )
8. (   )

Complete each sentence with an occupation.

_____ treats sick animals.

_____ writes programs for computers.

_____ collects news for newspapers or television.

_____ writes fiction stories.

Reading Water 29

Water is important. It covers about 70% of the Earth. About 60% to 75% of our body is water. Fresh water has no smell, taste or color. There are three states of water: liquid, solid and gas. Water starts freezing and becomes ice at 0 degrees Celsius. It starts boiling and becomes steam at 100 degrees Celsius. We use water in all three of its states.

Unit 4 2A

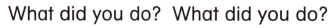

What did you do? What did you do?
What did you do while I was out?

Oh, no! Believe me, please!
I did not do anything bad!
I tried to clean the room for you.

You broke the vase.

I tried to cook dinner for you.

You broke the dish.

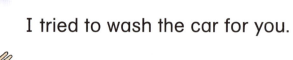

I tried to wash the car for you.

You crashed my car!

What did you do? What did you do?
What did you do while I was out?

Oh, no! Believe me, please!
I did not do anything bad!

2B

 🔊 32

play played	open opened	clean cleaned	live lived
love loved	smile smiled	believe believed	study studied
cry cried	try tried	walk walked	wash washed
crash crashed	watch watched	want wanted	visit visited
start started	stop stopped	drop dropped	plan planned

Unit 4

What I did last Sunday

One thing I did last Sunday:
_____
_____

Guess what I did!
Find out what each member in your group did.

Q1 Did you do this indoors or outdoors?

Q2 Did you do this at home? Where did you do this?

Q3 Did you do this with somebody? If yes, how many people did you do this with?

Q4 Did you need anything to do this? If yes, what did you need?

name	what he/she did

Two people who did something good

Did you do something good yesterday? Yes → What did you do? I ……

name	what you / he / she did
I	

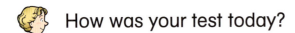

I failed the test.

- How was your test today?

- I failed.

- You failed the test? Didn't you study?

- Yes, I did. I studied for three hours last night.

- How? What did you do?

- Well, I read the English textbook aloud three times.

  I wrote all the new English words five times.

  And I memorized all the new English sentences.

- So why did you fail the test? Were you late?

- No. I got up early this morning and arrived at school early.

  But… the test was not an English test. It was a math test.

- Oh, no!!!!

3B

 🔊 35

get got   have had   tell told   meet met   buy bought   find found   make made
break broke   eat ate   give gave   go went   know knew   see saw   speak spoke
take took   write wrote   come came   cut cut   put put   feed fed   read read

Chores at home after school

Ask questions to identify the person, using "Did you …?"

Daichi
- ✓ vacuum the living room
- ☐ empty the trash cans
- ✓ water the flowers
- ✓ make a salad for dinner
- ✓ fold the laundry
- ✓ feed the fish

Eve
- ✓ vacuum the living room
- ✓ empty the trash cans
- ☐ water the flowers
- ✓ make a salad for dinner
- ☐ fold the laundry
- ✓ feed the fish

Claire
- ☐ vacuum the living room
- ✓ empty the trash cans
- ☐ water the flowers
- ✓ make a salad for dinner
- ✓ fold the laundry
- ✓ feed the fish

Tina
- ☐ vacuum the living room
- ✓ empty the trash cans
- ☐ water the flowers
- ☐ make a salad for dinner
- ✓ fold the laundry
- ✓ feed the fish

Ibuki
- ☐ vacuum the living room
- ✓ empty the trash cans
- ☐ water the flowers
- ✓ make a salad for dinner
- ☐ fold the laundry
- ✓ feed the fish

Nelson
- ☐ vacuum the living room
- ☐ empty the trash cans
- ✓ water the flowers
- ✓ make a salad for dinner
- ☐ fold the laundry
- ☐ feed the fish

Mary
- ✓ vacuum the living room
- ✓ empty the trash cans
- ☐ water the flowers
- ✓ make a salad for dinner
- ✓ fold the laundry
- ✓ feed the fish

Mark
- ☐ vacuum the living room
- ☐ empty the trash cans
- ✓ water the flowers
- ✓ make a salad for dinner
- ✓ fold the laundry
- ☐ feed the fish

Write three household chores that you regularly do at home.

1. _____
2. _____
3. _____

Write three more household chores that you think children should do at home.

1. _____
2. _____
3. _____

Unit 5 1A

36 → 37

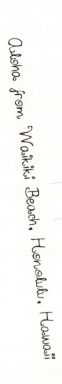

HAWAII Tuesday, August 20th

Dear Mom and Dad,
I arrived at Waikiki two days ago. Flying alone was a little scary, but fun! Uncle James came to meet me at the airport. He took me to the beach yesterday. We went jet skiing in the sea. We're going to hike to the top of the mountain tomorrow, and I'm looking forward to seeing the sunset from there. Thank you very much for letting me visit Uncle James.   Love, Daichi

Aloha from Waikiki Beach, Honolulu, Hawaii

1B Writing a postcard

Travel Itinerary

Destination: London　　**Period:** 5th – 13th September 20XX

Date	Activities
September 5th	✈ Leave Narita at 12:35 on flight #2071
	✈ Arrive at Heathrow Airport at 5:10 in the evening
September 6th	🏨 Stay in London Hotel near Hyde Park
September 7th	Visit Buckingham Palace. See the ceremony of the Changing of the Guard
	Visit the Tower of London and Big Ben in the afternoon
September 8th	Visit Stonehenge and Greenwich
September 9th	Visit the British Museum
September 10th	Take a one-day trip to the Lake District by train
	Visit the Peter Rabbit Museum
September 11th	🛍 Go shopping at Harrods
	Have afternoon tea
September 12th	✈ Leave Heathrow Airport at 3:30 in the afternoon
September 13th	✈ Arrive at Narita at 11:05 in the morning

Choose a date. You are writing this postcard at eight o'clock in the morning on that date.

- leave — left — be going to leave
- stay — stayed — be going to stay
- see — saw — be going to see
- go — went — be going to go
- arrive — arrived — be going to arrive
- visit — visited — be going to visit
- take — took — be going to take
- have — had — be going to have

I was a little tree in spring.

I was shorter than a flower.

I was the shortest tree in the forest.

But when summer came, I grew taller.

And when fall came, I grew taller.

When winter came, I grew taller.

Many springs, summers,
falls and winters came.

And now I am the tallest,
biggest and oldest tree in the forest.

2B Unit 5

I am happy.   I am happier.   I am the happiest.

Identify who is who

Q Are you Kelly? Are you taller than Kelly?

S's name										
Melvin										
Ken										
Jennifer										
Yoko										
Sue										
Rick										
Kelly										
David										
Mike										
Momoko										

Answers

_____ is Melvin.   _____ is Ken.

_____ is Jennifer.   _____ is Yoko.   _____ is Sue.

_____ is Rick.   _____ is Kelly.   _____ is David.

_____ is Mike.   _____ is Momoko.

Unit 5 3A

40

Aesop's Fables :
The Cow and the Frog

There once lived a little frog. One day the frog saw a big cow. The cow was eating grass in the field. The little frog was very surprised. It hopped all the way home to tell its mother. "Oh, Mother!" it cried. "There was a huge animal in the field. It was as big as a mountain!"

The mother frog took a deep breath to puff herself up. Soon she became as big as a basketball. "Am I bigger than the animal? Was the animal as big as I am now?" she asked. "Oh, no, it was much, much bigger!" said the little frog.

The mother frog took an even deeper breath and made herself puff up even more! Soon she was as big as a cat. "Was the animal as big as I am now?" she asked. "No, no. It was much, much bigger!" answered the little frog. "What!? Am I still smaller than the animal? I can't believe it!" the mother frog shouted. "Mother, you can do it," said the little frog. "OK. Watch me!"

Then she took the deepest breath she could, and she puffed and puffed. She became as big as a basketball, she became as big as a cat, and finally she became as big as a dog! And Boooooom!!! She popped!

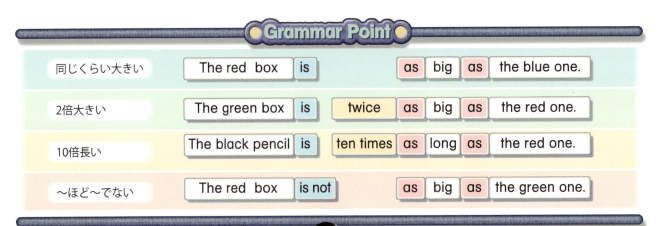

3B
Unit 5

🔊 41
A frog is as big as a ball. ××   A frog is as big as a cat. ××
A frog is as big as a dog. ××   Booooom!!!

| as big as a ball | as big as a cat | as big as a dog |

Five Pencils

Exchange information and complete the pencils.

Ⓐ
Ⓑ
Ⓒ
Ⓓ
Ⓔ

Countries by size

Choose the country and fill in the blanks.

Japan is the 60th biggest country of the 200 countries in the world.

1. _____ is as big as Japan.
2. _____ is almost 25 times as big as Japan.
3. _____ is almost 26 times as big as Japan.
4. _____ is almost 26 times as big as Japan.

Therefore, _____ is as big as _____.

5. _____ is 45 times as big as Japan.
6. _____ is smaller than Japan.

China   the USA   Russia   Canada   England   Germany

33
thirty-three

Unit 6 1A

 Are you ready to go to the station?

 I want to stop by a convenience store.

 What for?

 To buy something.

 Something?

 Yes. Something to drink.

 Is there anything else you want to do?

 I also want to go to the library.

 What for?

 To borrow a book.

 A book?

Yes. To read on the train.

 So, you want to stop by a convenience store to buy something to drink. And then, you want to go to the library to borrow a book to read on the train.

Yes, that's right.

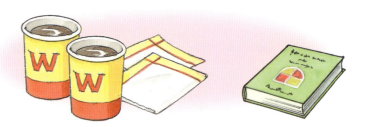

Grammar Point

I want **to stop by** a convenience store **to buy** something **to drink.**

〜すること   〜するために   〜するための

1B

Survey about school life

	It's reasonable …	me	agree	disagree
1	to wear a school uniform every day		|||||	|||||
2	to clean our classroom ourselves		|||||	|||||
3	to have homework during vacations		|||||	|||||
4	to clean the school toilets ourselves		|||||	|||||
5	to stand and bow at the beginning of each class		|||||	|||||

	It's acceptable …	me	acceptable	unacceptable
1	to dye our hair		|||||	|||||
2	to wear earrings to school		|||||	|||||
3	to wear make-up		|||||	|||||
4	to modify our uniform		|||||	|||||
5	not to join a club activity		|||||	|||||
6	not to go to school regularly		|||||	|||||
7	to buy something to eat on the way back from school		|||||	|||||

Speech: My school's regulations

There are many regulations in my school.

I (think / don't think) it is (reasonable / acceptable) to _____

because _____

_____ What do you think? Thank you.

Reading Plants   44

Many people want **to keep** plants in their room. But it is not easy **to grow** them. Plants need water, air, light and proper temperature **to grow**. In winter we need to cover some plants **to keep** them warm. Nutrients are also important **to make** big flowers, green leaves and strong roots.

35
thirty-five

Unit 6 2A

Listen to me. Listen to me.

I want you to study hard.

I'm listening. I'm listening.

I want you to leave me alone.

Listen to me. Listen to me.

I want you to clean your room.

I'm listening. I'm listening.

I want you to leave me alone.

Leave me alone. Leave me alone……

Listen to me. Listen to me……

Grammar Point

〜がほしい	I want	a bag.
〜したい	I want to	study English.
あなたに〜してもらいたい	I want you to	study English.

2B　　　　　　　　　　　　　　　　　　　　　Unit 6

Hopes and tasks in my life

want to (positive attitude) **/ have to** (negative attitude)

1 I _____ go to school.

2 I _____ do my homework.

3 I _____ take tests.

4 I _____ be nice to my grandparents.

5 I _____ clean my room.

6 I _____ offer my seat to the elderly in the train.

7 I _____ study at university.

8 I _____ work in the future.

want someone / don't want anyone

9 I _____ to help me with my homework.

10 I _____ to clean my room while I am out.

11 I _____ to read my diary.

12 I _____ to walk to school with me.

Speech: What I want to do in my life

Today I'll tell you three things I want to do in my life.

_____

_____

_____

_____

_____

_____

_____

_____ Thank you.

47→48

 I told you to do this. But you didn't do it.

 Really? Did you tell me?

 I told you not to do that. But you did it!

 Really? I didn't hear you.

49→50

 Tell me, tell me everything.

I don't know what to do.

I don't know where to go.

I don't know when to go.

I don't know how to go.

I don't know anything.

 I told you. I told you. I told you everything.

I told you not to go.

I told you not to go out.

I told you not to play today.

I told you to do your homework!

Grammar Point

何をするかを知っている。	I	know	what	to do.
どこに行くかを知っている。	I	know	where	to go.
いつ行くかを知っている。	I	know	when	to go.
どうやって行くかを知っている。	I	know	how	to go.
泳ぎ方を知っている。	I	know	how	to swim.
あなたに、これをするように言った。	I	told	you	to do this.
あなたに、あれはしないように言った。	I	told	you	not	to do that.

3B

How to get there

Ex. Excuse me. I want to go to the museum. Do you know how to get there?
Excuse me. I want to go surfing. Do you know where to go?
Yes … / Sorry, I'm a stranger here, too.

1 go surfing
Take bus No. _____.
Get off at the _____ stop.
The name of the bus stop is _____.

2 go skiing
Take bus No. _____.
Get off at the _____ stop.
The name of the bus stop is _____.

3 go on a picnic
Take bus No. _____.
Get off at the _____ stop.
The name of the bus stop is _____.

4 go to the museum
Take bus No. _____.
Get off at the _____ stop.
The name of the bus stop is _____.

5 go to the aquarium
Take bus No. _____.
Get off at the _____ stop.
The name of the bus stop is _____.

6 go to the concert hall
Take bus No. _____.
Get off at the _____ stop.
The name of the bus stop is _____.

7 go to the shopping mall
Take bus No. _____.
Get off at the _____ stop.
The name of the bus stop is _____.

Write about yourself

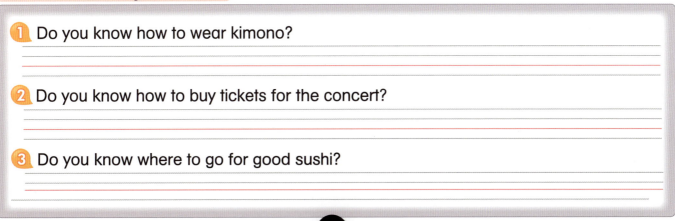

1. Do you know how to wear kimono?
   _____
   _____

2. Do you know how to buy tickets for the concert?
   _____
   _____

3. Do you know where to go for good sushi?
   _____
   _____

51→52

 I have to give a speech in class next week.

Will you give me some advice so that I can give a good speech?

 OK. First of all, you should choose a good topic.

Then, you should go to the library to get more information on your topic.

You'd better not get all your information only from websites.

Some of the information on them may be wrong.

 All right. What should I do after I write my script?

 You have to prepare well and practice hard.

If I were you, I'd practice reading the script in front of a mirror.

You've got to be confident in front of the audience.

 Do I have to memorize my script?

 Yes. You mustn't read your script. You should stand straight and

keep your head up. You have to look around the room and try to

make eye contact with everyone.

 It is difficult, isn't it?

 Yes, it is. You should try to speak not too fast but loudly, clearly and slowly.

Oh, yes. And looking friendly and smiling is also very important.

 OK, I'll try my best.

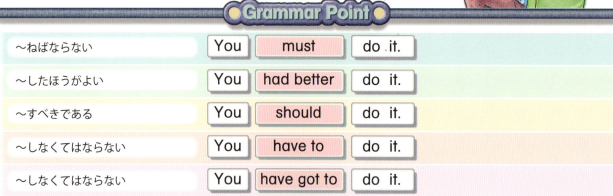

〜ねばならない	You	must	do it.
〜したほうがよい	You	had better	do it.
〜すべきである	You	should	do it.
〜しなくてはならない	You	have to	do it.
〜しなくてはならない	You	have got to	do it.

1B Unit 7

  53

You should do it, you must do it, you'd better do it, I tell you!
We should do it, we must do it, we'd better do it, I tell you!

Giving your friend advice

Give your friend advice using "**must, should, have to** and **had better**".

1 I have a fever.
You _____

If I were you, I would _____

2 I can't sleep well.
You _____

If I were you, I would _____

3 I lost my smartphone.
You _____

If I were you, I would _____

go to bed early　not stay up late　see a doctor　get some exercise　drink a lot of water
take some medicine　tell your mother　stay in bed　go to the police station　give up
go to the lost and found counter　not take a bath　take a warm bath　not eat sweets
go back home to get it　eat a lot of vegetables　buy a new one　your own advice

Speech: What I should do to improve my English skills

In order to be able to use English well, I think

I should _____.

I should _____

And I should _____.

I will do my best! Thank you.

54→55

If you are free, please come around.
If it is fine, you can walk to my house.
If you get lost, you can call me.
If it is rainy, take bus No. 4.
If you are hungry, I'll make you lunch.
And if it is hot, let's go swimming after lunch.

Thank you, Aunty.
If I were free, I'd be happy to come over.
But I'm afraid I can't.
I wish I could.
Sorry...

Grammar Point

「If... もしも…」

■「起こりうる『もしも』とそれに続いて起こること」Real possibility

もし、このボタンを押したらドアが開くでしょう。　| If | you | press | this button, | the door | will | open. |

■「想像される『もしも』と、その結果起こるだろうと思われること」Imagine something

もし、このボタンを押したらモンスターが現れるかも。　| If | I | pressed | this button, | a monster | would | appear. |

■「今はできないけれど、できたらいいなぁと思うこと」

飛べたらなあ。　| I | wish | I | could | fly. |　　きみがぼくを助けてくれたらなあ。　| I | wish | you | would | help | me. |

2B Unit 7

  56

If it is OK, I will go.   If it is not, I won't go.
If you were there, I'd go there.

Quiz
A train runs through a tunnel. We cannot see the train for 15 seconds. If the length of the tunnel is 400 meters and the length of the train is 100 meters, how fast does this train run per second?

Imagine what you would do if ...

Choose what you would do in each situation.

1 If I found a fifty yen coin on the street,
I would ☐ take it to the police box.   ☐ put it in my pocket.
☐ buy something for myself.   ☐ donate it.   ☐ leave it there.
☐ _____

2 If I found a ten thousand yen bill on the street,
I would ☐ take it to the police box.   ☐ put it in my pocket.
☐ buy something for myself.   ☐ donate it.   ☐ leave it there.
☐ _____

3 If an old person were standing in front of me on the train,
I would ☐ offer my seat.   ☐ sleep.   ☐ play a video game.
☐ read a book.   ☐ do nothing.
☐ _____

4 Choose one famous person (a singer, an actress, an actor) and write his or her name.
If I met _____
I would ☐ ask for his/her signature. ☐ talk to him/her. ☐ take a photo with my cell phone.
☐ ask to shake hands.   ☐ have a picture taken with him/her.   ☐ do nothing.
☐ _____

I wish I could ...

I wish I could _____
_____
_____
_____ .

Show and Tell

Hello, everybody.
Today I'm going to show you a picture of my sister and tell you a funny little story about her.

As you know, I have a sister called Ibuki. This is her and her favorite toy. Our grandmother gave her this toy on her second birthday. Ibuki was very happy to get it. Grandmother showed her how to play with it. Ibuki just loved jumping on it. Boing, boing, boing, like in a rodeo. She jumped with it all day long. She named it Boing Boing Roba-san. Roba-san means Mr. Donkey in Japanese. She loved the toy and its name very much.

Well, I wanted to jump on Roba-san, too, but she wouldn't let me use it. So I decided to do something mean to her. One day, I told her the truth! That is, the toy was not a donkey, but a horse. And I showed her a picture of a donkey and a picture of a horse. She was very shocked to know the truth. Ibuki is eight years old now. She still calls it Boing Boing Roba-san and still will not let me use it.
Thank you.

Grammar Point

あなたに本を見せましょう。	I'll	show	you	a book.
あなたに本をあげましょう。	I'll	give	you	a book.
あなたに道を教えましょう。	I'll	tell	you	the way.
あなたに英語を教えましょう。	I'll	teach	you	English.
あなたにケーキを作りましょう。	I'll	make	you	a cake.
あなたに本を買いましょう。	I'll	buy	you	a book.

Unit 7

  59

Show me this. Show me that. Show me everything.
Give me this. Give me that. Give me everything.

Show and tell

Speech: My favorite gift

Today I will show you my _____,
and tell you a little story about it.

_____
_____
_____
_____
_____
_____
_____
_____
_____
_____
_____
_____   Thank you.

Who or what?

1 _____ teaches us English.

2 _____ teaches us Home Economics.

3 _____ taught me how to swim.

4 _____ gave me the best present.

5 _____ gives me presents at Christmas every year.

6 _____ always tells me what to do and what not to do.

7 I have a very good friend.
   I will give him/her _____ on his/her birthday.

Unit 8 1A

 Look at that man!

 Which one?

 The man wearing a bright pink sweater.

 Oh, that's my father!

 Look at that man!

 Which one?

 The man crossing the street against the red light.

 Oh, no! That's my teacher!

 Look at that man!

 Which one?

 The man carrying a pretty red bag.

 Oh, no! That's my bag!

●Grammar Point●

あの犬を見て。	Look at	the		dog.
あの寝ている犬を見て。	Look at	the	sleeping	dog.
あのベンチの上で寝ている犬を見て。	Look at	the		dog sleeping on the bench.

1B Unit 8

🎵 62

The dog running with a boy, the dog walking with a girl,
The dog sleeping on the bench, the dog chasing a cat!

Identify the dogs

Exchange information and write the names of each dog.

Q That's Wincey. Which one? The dog running with a boy is Wincey. How do you spell Wincey?

Choose one dog and describe it.   **Ex.** The dog running with a boy is Wincey.

The dog _____ is _____

🎵 63

Reading: Venus

The star shining brightly in the west just after the sun sets is Venus.
Venus is called the evening star when it appears in the west just after sunset.
The star shining brightly in the east just before the sun rises is Venus, too.
Venus is called the morning star when it appears in the east just before sunrise.
The star called the evening star and the star called the morning star are both Venus.

Unit 8 2A

Which bird?

A bird.
A red bird.

A bird.
A big bird.

A bird.
A bird in the tree.

A bird.
A bird flying over there.

A bird.
A bird which comes to Japan.

A bird.
A bird whose beak is yellow.

A bird.
A bird which you bought.

Grammar Point

鳥	a bird		
日本に飛来する鳥	a bird	which	comes to Japan.
くちばしが黄色い鳥	a bird	whose	beak is yellow.
あなたが買った鳥	a bird	which	you bought.

2B Unit 8

  66

A bird, a yellow bird singing a sweet song.
A bird, a big bird whose eyes are green.
A bird, a cute bird (which) I love so much.
A bird, a naughty bird which broke the cage!

Characters from Fairy Tales

Write the name.

1. The princess who lived with seven dwarves and ate a poisoned apple is
( )

2. The princess who had shoes made of glass and rode in a carriage made from a big pumpkin is
( )

3. The boy who was born from a peach and had a monkey, a dog, and a pheasant as friends is
( )

4. The boy who saved a turtle and went to a castle under the sea is
( )

5. The girl whose parents live on the moon is
( )

6. The boy whose nose grew long when he told a lie is
( )

7. The country where Peter Pan came from is
( )

Story Writing

This is the story of _____ (which / whose) _____ .

Unit 8 3A

67  68→69

This is a famous story which everyone in Japan knows.

The story is about a boy who was born from a peach.

Once upon a time, there was an old couple who lived in a small village.

They had a small house which was on the hill.

One day, the old man went to the mountain where he gathered firewood.

The old lady went to the river where she washed their clothes.

There she found a big peach which was floating down the stream.

The old lady took the big peach home….

Grammar Point

男の子	the boy		
桃から生まれた男の子	the boy	who	was born from a peach
家	the house		
丘の上の家（家を物と考えた場合）	the house	which	was on the hill
彼が住んでいる家（家を場所と考えた場合）	the house	where	he lives

50
fifty

3B   Unit 8

  70

This is the boy who(m) I love.   This is the boy who loves me.
This is the house which I built. This is the house where I live.   Well... life is not easy.

Find someone who...

		name	What kind	Why
Ex	likes music	Tom	pop music	exciting
1	enjoys reading books			
2	likes watching sports			
3	is collecting something			
			Where	Why
4	wants to go abroad			

Ex Someone who likes music is Tom. He likes pop music because it is exciting.

1 Someone who enjoys reading books is _____

He/She likes _____ because _____

2 Someone who likes watching sports is _____

He/She likes watching _____ because _____

3 Someone who is collecting something is _____

He/She is collecting _____ because _____

4 Someone who wants to go abroad is _____

He/She wants to go to _____ because _____

Quiz

❶ This is the man who officially established the shogunate in Edo on March 24th in 1603.

The man who started the Edo period is (　　　　　　　).

❷ This is music which Beethoven composed.

This music, which Beethoven composed, is Symphony No.(　　　).

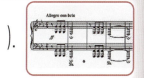

 Unit 9 1A

 71→72

Have you seen the new bridge?

No. Not yet.

Really? You should see it. It's huge!

 73→74

Have you seen it?   Have you seen it?

No, I haven't.   No, I haven't.

You should see it.   It's so cool!

Have you been there?   Have you been there?

No, I haven't.   No, I haven't.

You should go there.   It's so great!

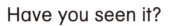 Grammar Point

1B　　　　　　　　　　　　　　　　　　　　　　　　　　　Unit 9

  75

食べる	食べた	食べちゃった		行く	行った	行っちゃった
eat	ate	have eaten		go	went	have gone

取る	取った	取っちゃった		見る	見た	見ちゃった		する	した	しちゃった
take	took	have taken		see	saw	have seen		do	did	have done

What I have done so far

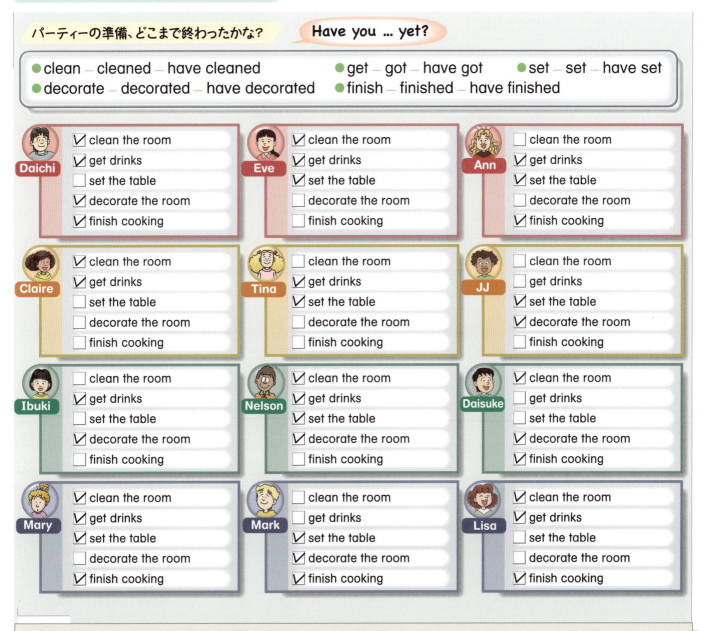

Fill in the blanks with your recommendation and the reason for it.

A: Have you (seen / been to) _____?

B: No, I haven't.

A: You should (see it / go there). It's so great!

B: What's so great?

A: _____.

76→77

 Look at this picture. I drew a chicken.

 A chicken doesn't have four legs!

 You're right. A chicken has only two legs.

 I've never seen a chicken with four legs.

78→79

Have you ever seen a snake,
   a snake with legs?　　　　NEVER.

Have you ever seen a pig,
   a pig with wings?　　　　NEVER.

Have you ever seen a zebra,
   a zebra without stripes?　　NEVER!

Grammar Point

～を見たことがありますか。	Have you (ever) seen a ghost?
おばけを見たことがあります。	I have seen a ghost.
おばけを見たことがありません。	I have never seen a ghost.

54
fifty-four

2B

Unit 9

  80

Never? Ever? You've never been there?   Oh, you're kidding!
Never? Ever? You've never seen it?   I can't believe it!

Exciting Experiences

About myself

1	I (have / haven't) met a famous person.
2	I (have / haven't) been on TV.
3	I (have / haven't) ridden a horse.
4	I (have / haven't) seen a shooting star.
5	I (have / haven't) stayed up all night.

Find someone who

A: Have you ever met a famous person?
B: Yes, I have. I met …

	name	When? How?
1		
2		
3		
4		

Speech: An exciting thing that happened in my life

Choose one of the "yes" answers from the above topics and make a speech.
When was it?   How many times?   How did it happen?   How did you feel?   What did you do next?

Have you ever _____?

I have _____

_____

Thank you.

 Have you ever been abroad?

 No, I have never been abroad. Have you?

 Yes, I have. Let me show you some pictures I took in Hawaii.

 Sure.

 Hawaii is the most amazing place I've ever been to.

This is the most beautiful sunset I've ever seen.

This is the biggest shopping center I've ever been to.

And these are the best pancakes I've ever had!

 They look good!

Grammar Point

ぼくが今まで食べた一番大きなアイスクリーム	the	biggest	ice cream	(that)	I have ever had
ぼくが今まで見た一番きれいな夕日	the	most	beautiful sunset	(that)	I have ever seen

3B   Unit 9

 83

> You are the nicest teacher I've ever met.
> You are the most thoughtful teacher I've ever met.
> You are the most wonderful teacher I've ever met. So please…

The most … in my life

1. The funniest person I have ever met:
2. The most beautiful sight I have ever seen:
3. The best place I have ever been to:
4. The greatest person I have ever met:
5. The most difficult kanji I have ever learned:

   Write it.

6. The easiest cartoon character to draw:

   Draw it.

Speech: The most … in my life

Choose one of the above topics 1-4 and make a speech.

The _____ I've ever _____

is _____.

_____

Thank you.

Unit 10 1A

84→85

 I'm sorry to have kept you waiting.
I've been busy all day today.
Where have you been?
I've been waiting for you for two hours!

86→87
Where have you been?
Where have you been?
I've been waiting for you.

Where have you been?
Where have you been?
I've been looking for you.

How have you been?
How have you been?
I've been worrying about you.

Grammar Point

英語を勉強します。	I	study	English.	
英語を勉強しました。	I	studied	English.	
英語を勉強するつもりです。	I	will study	English.	
今英語の勉強をしています。	I	am studying	English.	now.
英語の勉強をしたことがあります。	I	have studied	English.	
5歳の時から7年間英語の勉強をしています。	I	have been studying	English.	for seven years / since I was five.

1B Unit 10

  88 *I've been tired. I've been sick. I haven't had anything since last night.*

What I've been doing

About myself

1. I've been studying English for _____ years since _____.
2. I've lived in my current home for _____ years since _____.
3. I've been good friends with _____ for _____ years since _____.

since… (I was born. / I was __ years old. / I was in the __ grade.)

Ask your partner

1. Q When did you start studying English?   When I was _____.
   Q How long have you been studying English?   For _____ years.
   _____ has been studying English for _____ years since _____.

2. Q When did you start living in your current home?   When I was _____.
   Q How long have you been living there?   For _____ years.
   _____ has been living in his/her current home for ____ years since _____.

3. Q Who is one of your best friends?   _____
   Q When did you first meet him/her?   When I was _____.
   Q How long have you known him/her?   For _____ years.
   _____ has been friends with _____ for ____ years since _____.

Quiz

❶ He started playing the game at seven o'clock. It is ten now.
   How long has he been playing the game?
For (   ) hours!

❷ My sister went to bed at eight o'clock last night.
   It's already ten o'clock in the morning. She is still sleeping!
How long has she been sleeping?   For (   ) hours!

Jack and the Beanstalk

"This tiny seed will give you hope and happiness, hope for a better life, hope for tomorrow. If you exchange your cow for this seed, you and your mother will surely be happier."

An old man told Jack this on the way to the market. Jack was going to the market to sell the cow. He wanted to **make his mother happy**. So he gave the cow to the old man and got a tiny seed. "What? You did not go to the market? You did not sell the cow? And you got this seed in place of that cow?" His mother burst into tears. She threw the seed out of the window. Jack was so sorry that he had exchanged the cow for that tiny seed. But… during the night, the seed began to grow. It got taller and taller and became a big beanstalk! The top of the beanstalk was higher than a cloud!

"Mom, I want to climb the beanstalk. I want to know what is up there. I believe there is something, something that will **make us happy**, just as the old man told me."

Then Jack started climbing the tall beanstalk.

What do you think Jack will find up there?

Grammar Point

私は	お母さんを	幸せに	する	I	make	my mother	happy.
私は	彼を	ジュンと	呼ぶ	I	call	him	Jun.
私は	それを	タマと	名付けた	I	named	it	Tama.

2B
Unit 10

 90 A dog is running. A dog is running. That's my dog.
I love my dog. I love my dog. So I give him a bone. That makes him happy.

What makes you happy

Write five things that make you happy.

_____ , _____ , _____ ,

_____ , and _____ make me happy.

Write three things that make people happy at each age.

5 months old			
6 years old			
25 years old			
50 years old			
80 years old			

Write your own answers.

1. If I get a puppy and it is a girl, I'll name it _____ .

2. It is (easy / difficult) to keep my room clean and tidy.

3. What should you do to make your (mother, friend, teacher) happy?
   _____

What do you think Jack will find up there?

I think he will find _____ .

 Look! This wine is made by my father.

 Really? Let me try.

 No, no. You cannot drink wine!

💿 93→94

The wine is made, made from grapes.

The hill is covered, covered with vines.

The vine is full, full of grapes.

The grapes are cut, cut by a farmer.

The barrel is filled, filled with grapes.

The barrel is made, made of wood.

Everyone is pleased, pleased with the wine.

The wine is known, known to everyone.

Grammar Point

~される…

| 話される言語（＝話し言葉） | Spoken | language | | |
| そこで話される言語は英語です。 | The | language | spoken there | is English. |

…は～ されています。

| 多くの人が英語を話します。 | Many people | | speak | English. |
| 英語は多くの人によって話されています。 | English | is | spoken | by | many people. |

3B

  95

Unit 10

see saw seen, speak spoke spoken, take took taken, write wrote written,
give gave given, know knew known, draw drew drawn, eat ate eaten,
make made made, tell told told, meet met met, find found found,
buy bought bought, bring brought brought, catch caught caught, have had had,
keep kept kept, sell sold sold, send sent sent, cut cut cut!

This passage written here is...

❶ Τι κάνεις ( )

❸ Cześć, co słychać? ( )

❺ 你好嗎？ ( )

❷ สบายดีหรือ ( )

❹ Как вы поживáете? ( )

❻ 잘 지내세요? ( )

Russian   Chinese   Greek   Thai   Polish   Korean

These structures are made of ...   paper mud stones bricks ice wood straw sand

❶ This house is made of _____.
❷ This house is made of _____.
❸ This church is made of _____.
❹ This temple is made of _____.
❺ This house is made of _____.
❻ This house is made of _____.
❼ This nest is made of _____.
❽ This house is made of _____.

I want to live in a house which is made of _____.

This passage is spoken in

❶ _____   ❷ _____   ❸ _____   ❹ _____

a: Spanish
b: Korean
c: Thai
d: German

supplement  Listening Test

Unit 1

1
a. Daichi.
b. Asahi.
c. My last name.

2
a. My friends.
b. School band.
c. Trumpet.

3
a. To live in Hawaii.
b. To live in Australia.
c. To have a big family.

Look at page 7. Write the correct number.

4

5

6

7
a. Asahi.
b. Sunflower
c. Mr. Mayor.

8
a. more than 354,000
b. less than 354,000
c. 354,000

9
a. Yes, there is.
b. No, there isn't.
c. Yes, it does.

Unit 2

1
a. It's cold.
b. Hot cocoa.
c. Cold cocoa.

2
a. Through Ken.
b. By letter.
c. By e-mail.

3
a. Lions.
b. Zebras.
c. Pandas.

4
a. 1500 grams.
b. 1 km/hour.
c. 70 km/hour.

5
a. Yes, they are.
b. Yes, they can.
c. Yes, they do.

6
a. I am a Cat.
b. English literature.
c. London.

7
a. A clock.
b. A picture.
c. A TV.

8
a. She is reading the newspaper.
b. He is reading a book.
c. She is watching TV.

9
a. One.
b. Two.
c. Three.

64
sixty-four

Listening Test

Unit 3

1
a. Fallen leaves.
b. Fall.
c. Colored leaves.

2
a. Every Wednesday.
b. Once a month.
c. Twice a month.

3
a. She is eating eggs.
b. She is going to bury them.
c. She is cleaning egg shells.

4
a. She is sick.
b. She broke her leg.
c. She is going to the hospital.

5
a. She is going to high school.
b. She is going to study in England.
c. She is going to be a teacher.

6
a. To study.
b. By train.
c. To City Hall.

7
a. Because he is with his friend.
b. Because his family has another plan.
c. Because his uncle James is coming to visit him.

8
a. Because it was too bright.
b. Because it was pretty.
c. Because it was blue.

9
a. Because he has got a lot of new friends.
b. Because it was good to meet his old friend.
c. Because he has a lot of homework every day.

Unit 4

Look at page 23. Write the correct number.

1

2

3

4
a. He stayed home.
b. He went to see a basketball game.
c. He went fishing with his father.

5
a. He cleaned his room.
b. He studied for the test.
c. He had a science test.

6
a. In the supermarket.
b. This afternoon.
c. Terry.

Look at page 27. Write his/her name.

7

8

9

supplement Listening Test

Unit 5

1
a. Summer vacation.
b. Peter Rabbit Museum.
c. London.

2
a. Narita Airport.
b. Heathrow Airport.
c. Euston Station.

Look at page 31.
3
a. Mike.
b. David.
c. Sue.

Look at page 31.
4
a. Ken.
b. Melvin.
c. Rick.

5
a. The red pencil.
b. The green pencil.
c. The brown pencil.

6
a. The boy's ticket was cheaper.
b. The girl's ticket was cheaper.
c. They were the same price.

Unit 6

1
a. A convenience store.
b. A comic book.
c. A train.

2
a. Clean her room.
b. Write a letter.
c. Go to a party.

3
a. A cookie.
b. Hot cocoa.
c. Chicken noodle soup.

4
a. Yes, she does.
b. No, she doesn't.
c. She likes something else.

5
a. Students have their own classrooms.
b. Teachers have their own classrooms.
c. Teachers stand and bow.

6
a. Go scuba diving.
b. Go swimming.
c. Go sightseeing.

Unit 7

1
a. At three o'clock.
b. At seven o'clock.
c. At ten o'clock.

2
a. A script.
b. His favorite books.
c. Keeping his head up.

3
a. To church.
b. To wear the red dress.
c. To the library.

4
a. It depends.
b. Put it in his pocket.
c. Take it to the police box.

5
a. A sweater.
b. A bag.
c. A sweater and a bag.

6
a. Ms. Sasaki.
b. Mr. Baker.
c. Australian.

Listening Test

Unit 8

Look at page 47. Write the correct number.

1. _____
2. _____
3. _____

4.
a. How to play the piano.
b. How to go to France.
c. A piano teacher.

5.
a. Old coins.
b. Mrs. Jackson.
c. Stamps.

6.
a. Jack's family name is Smith.
b. The girl's father ran the city marathon.
c. The marathon was this year.

Unit 9

Look at page 53. Write his/her name.

1. _____
2. _____
3. _____

4.
a. Two times.
b. Never.
c. Guam.

5.
a. The boy has stayed up all night.
b. The girl has stayed up all night.
c. They both have seen shooting stars.

6.
a. In Hawaii.
b. At a language school.
c. Last year.

Unit 10

1.
a. The funniest person.
b. Since they were ten years old.
c. For ten years.

2.
a. Thank you.
b. For about 5 years.
c. It's good English.

3.
a. Puppy.
b. Elizabeth.
c. Beth.

4.
a. In front of the station.
b. Inside the station.
c. For thirty minutes.

5.
a. Bone.
b. Steel.
c. Wood.

6.
a. The house made of straw.
b. The house made of wood.
c. The house made of bricks.

supplement Irregular verbs

No.	meanings	Present	Past	Past Participle
1		be	was / were	been
2		bear	bore	born / borne
3		become	became	become
4		begin	began	begun
5		blow	blew	blown
6		break	broke	broken
7		bring	brought	brought
8		build	built	built
9		burn	burned / burnt	burned / burnt
10		buy	bought	bought
11		catch	caught	caught
12		choose	chose	chosen
13		come	came	come
14		cost	cost	cost
15		cut	cut	cut
16		do	did	done
17		draw	drew	drawn
18		dream	dreamed / dreamt	dreamed / dreamt
19		drink	drank	drunk
20		drive	drove	driven
21		eat	ate	eaten
22		fall	fell	fallen
23		feed	fed	fed
24		feel	felt	felt
25		fight	fought	fought
26		find	found	found
27		fly	flew	flown
28		forget	forgot	forgot / forgotten
29		forgive	forgave	forgiven
30		get	got	got / gotten
31		give	gave	given
32		go	went	gone
33		grow	grew	grown
34		hang	hung	hung
35		have	had	had
36		hear	heard	heard
37		hide	hid	hidden
38		hit	hit	hit
39		hold	held	held
40		hurt	hurt	hurt
41		keep	kept	kept
42		know	knew	known
43		lay	laid	laid
44		lead	led	led
45		learn	learned / learnt	learned / learnt
46		leave	left	left
47		lend	lent	lent
48		let	let	let
49		lie	lay	lain
50		lose	lost	lost

Irregular verbs

No.	meanings	Present	Past	Past Participle
51		make	made	made
52		mean	meant	meant
53		meet	met	met
54		mistake	mistook	mistaken
55		overcome	overcame	overcome
56		pay	paid	paid
57		put	put	put
58		quit	quit	quit
59		read	read	read
60		ride	rode	ridden
61		ring	rang	rung
62		rise	rose	risen
63		run	ran	run
64		say	said	said
65		see	saw	seen
66		seek	sought	sought
67		sell	sold	sold
68		send	sent	sent
69		set	set	set
70		shake	shook	shaken
71		shine	shone	shone
72		shoot	shot	shot
73		show	showed	shown
74		shut	shut	shut
75		sing	sang	sung
76		sink	sank	sunk
77		sit	sat	sat
78		sleep	slept	slept
79		slide	slid	slid / slidden
80		smell	smelled/smelt	smelled / smelt
81		speak	spoke	spoken
82		spell	spelled/spelt	spelled / spelt
83		spend	spent	spent
84		split	split	split
85		spread	spread	spread
86		stand	stood	stood
87		steal	stole	stolen
88		swim	swam	swum
89		swing	swung	swung
90		take	took	taken
91		teach	taught	taught
92		tell	told	told
93		think	thought	thought
94		throw	threw	thrown
95		understand	understood	understood
96		wake	woke	woken
97		wear	wore	worn
98		weep	wept	wept
99		win	won	won
100		write	wrote	written

supplement Grammer point

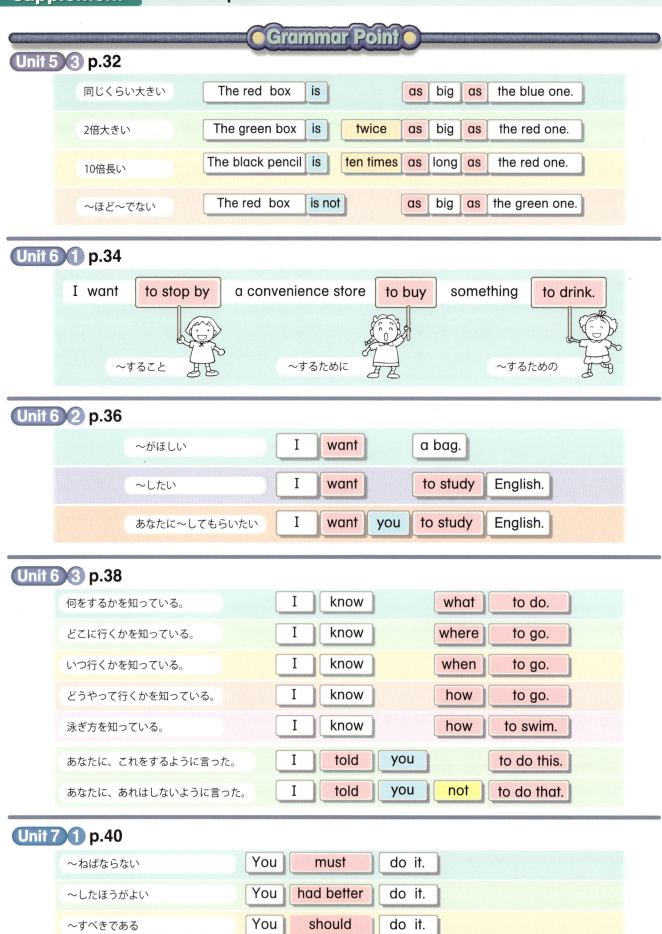

Grammar Point

Unit 7 2 p.42 「If... もしも…」

■ 「起こりうる『もしも』と、それに続いて起こること」Real possibility

もし、このボタンを押したらドアが開くでしょう。 If you press this button, the door will open.

■ 「想像される『もしも』と、その結果起こるだろうと思われること」Imagine something

もし、このボタンを押したらモンスターが現れるかも。 If I pressed this button, a monster would appear.

■ 「今はできないけれど、できたらいいなぁと思うこと」

飛べたらなあ。 I wish I could fly.　　きみがぼくを助けてくれたらなあ。 I wish you would help me.

Unit 7 3 p.44

あなたに本を見せましょう。	I'll	show	you	a book.
あなたに本をあげましょう。	I'll	give	you	a book.
あなたに道を教えましょう。	I'll	tell	you	the way.
あなたに英語を教えましょう。	I'll	teach	you	English.
あなたにケーキを作りましょう。	I'll	make	you	a cake.
あなたに本を買いましょう。	I'll	buy	you	a book.

Unit 8 1 p.46

あの犬を見て。	Look at the dog.
あの寝ている犬を見て。	Look at the sleeping dog.
あのベンチの上で寝ている犬を見て。	Look at the dog sleeping on the bench.

Unit 8 2 p.48

鳥	a bird
日本に飛来する鳥	a bird which comes to Japan.
くちばしが黄色い鳥	a bird whose beak is yellow.
あなたが買った鳥	a bird which you bought.

Unit 8 3 p.50

男の子	the boy
桃から生まれた男の子	the boy who was born from a peach
家	the house
丘の上の家（家を物と考えた場合）	the house which was on the hill
彼が住んでいる家（家を場所と考えた場合）	the house where he lives

71
seventy-one

supplement Grammer point

Grammar Point

Unit 9 ① p.52

| I | do | it. |

します

| I | did | it. |

しました

| I | have | (already) | done | it. |

（もう）しちゃった。

| I | haven't | done | it | (yet). |

（まだ）してません。

Unit 9 ② p.54

〜を見たことがありますか。 Have you (ever) seen a ghost?

おばけを見たことがあります。 I have seen a ghost.

おばけを見たことがありません。 I have never seen a ghost.

Unit 9 ③ p.56

ぼくが今まで食べた一番大きなアイスクリーム the biggest ice cream (that) I have ever had

ぼくが今まで見た一番きれいな夕日 the most beautiful sunset (that) I have ever seen

Unit 10 ① p.58

英語を勉強します。	I	study	English.
英語を勉強しました。	I	studied	English.
英語を勉強するつもりです。	I	will study	English.
今英語の勉強をしています。	I	am studying	English	now.
英語の勉強をしたことがあります。	I	have studied	English.
5歳の時から7年間英語の勉強をしています。	I	have been studying	English	for seven years	since I was five.

Unit 10 ② p.60

〜を 〜に する
私は お母さんを 幸せに する   I make my mother happy.

〜を 〜と 呼ぶ
私は 彼を ジュンと 呼ぶ   I call him Jun.

〜を 〜と 名付ける
私は それを タマと 名付けた   I named it Tama.

Unit 10 ③ p.62

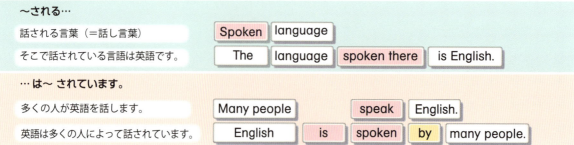

〜される…

話される言葉（＝話し言葉）   Spoken language

そこで話されている言語は英語です。   The language spoken there is English.

…は〜されています。

多くの人が英語を話します。   Many people speak English.

英語は多くの人によって話されています。   English is spoken by many people.

Words and Phrases Glossary

Unit 1-1 Me Myself 大地の自己紹介

introduce	～を紹介する
an office worker	事務員
a musical instrument	楽器
being alone	1人（ぼっち）でいる
blood	血
heights	高さ
thunderstorms	嵐、雷雨
gardening	庭いじり、園芸
being on my own	ひとりでいること
organized (person)	計画性のある(人)、物事をきちんとする(人)
intelligent	聡明な、(高度な)知性のある
good listener	聞き上手な
famous	有名な

Unit 1-2 The Beautiful Planet 美しい惑星―地球―

go(es) around	まわりをまわる
spin(s) around	軸を中心にまわる
cause(s)	(ある結果を)引き起こす
identify	～と見分ける
axis	軸
face (facing)	～に面する(面している)
light	光
heat	熱
daytime	昼間
is (be) tilted	傾いた

Unit 1-3 The Mayor's Speech 市長演説

mayor	市長
brave	勇敢な
population	人口
kindergarten(s)	幼稚園
are (be) proud of	～を誇りに思う
music hall	ミュージックホール、演芸場
fire station	消防署
amusement park	遊園地
smart	頭の良い、賢明な
shy	恥ずかしがりやの、内気な
sincere	誠実な
adventurous	大胆な、冒険好きな
athletic	筋骨たくましい
tough	頑丈な、タフな
optimistic	楽観的な
energetic	精力的な、エネルギッシュな
honest	正直な
ambitious	野心的な、意欲的な
humorous	ユーモアのある
unique	ユニークな、他に類を見ない

Unit 2-1 Hello. Come in. Help yourself. お友達の家へ

Help yourself.	ご自由にどうぞ。
Say hello to～.	～によろしくと言う(伝える)
keep in touch	連絡を取り合う
rinse	すすぐ、洗い落とす
drain	(水を)徐々に流す
several times	数回

button	ボタン
beep	ビーッという音を出す
is done	(ごはんが)炊き上がる
rice cooker	炊飯器
add	加える、追加する
automatically	自動的に
switch	切り替わる
measure	測る
surprising	驚くべき
taste	味がわかる

Unit 2-2 Surprising Facts おどろくべき動物たち

remember	(～を)覚えている、記憶している
for years	何年も
squid(s)	イカ
heart(s)	心臓
male	(動物の)オス
give birth	赤ちゃんを産む
weigh	重さが～である
fact(s)	事実
caterpillar	毛虫
leaves (leaf)	葉っぱ
mud	泥; ぬかるみ

Unit 2-3 My Past, Present and Future ぼくの過去・現在・未来

tadpole	おたまじゃくし
pond	池
astronaut	宇宙飛行士
space	宇宙

Unit 3-1 Recycling Garbage リサイクルを考える

plastic bag(s)	ビニール袋
styrofoam tray(s)	発泡スチロールのトレー
garbage	生ごみ
kitchen scraps	食べ残し、残飯
yard trimming(s)	庭ごみ
empty	〈容器など〉中身のない、空(から)の
flatten	平らにした
rinse	すすぐ、ゆすぐ
bin	ごみ入れ、ごみ箱
cardboard box	段ボール箱
flyer(s)	チラシ
junk mail	迷惑メール(ゴミ箱行きの郵便物)
egg shell(s)	卵の殻
dish soap	食器用洗剤
skin(s)	(野菜の薄い)皮
lid(s)	(容器などの)ふた
container(s)	容器、入れ物
jar(s)	(広口の)瓶
envelope(s)	封筒
beer	ビール
reusable	再利用可能な
less	より少ない
bottled	瓶の
donate	寄付する
follow	従う

supplement — Words and Phrases Glossary

recycling policies	リサイクル政策
instead of ~	~の代わりに

Unit 3-2 Starting off on a World Trip 世界旅行プラン

Ganges River	ガンジス川
Turkey	トルコ（共和国）
cave	洞窟
ibex	アイベックス《アルプス・ピレネー山脈などに住む野生ヤギ》
Algeria	アルジェリア
camel	ラクダ
Sahara Desert	サハラ砂漠
Colosseum	コロセウム（ローマの円形大演技場）
Venezuela	ベネズエラ
Angel Falls	アンヘル滝（落差が世界最大979m）
transportation	乗り物、輸送手段
itinerary	旅行プラン、旅程
route	ルート、経路

Unit 3-3 Asking Permission もう、十分な年齢です

by yourself	あなた一人で
too ~ to...	あまりに~なので...できない
too young	若すぎる
old enough to~	~してもよい年齢である
get along with~	~と仲良くする
behave yourself	行儀よくする
choose	選ぶ

Unit 4-1 My Routine Activities ぼくと妹の日課

occupation	職業
treat	治療する
liquid	液体
solid	固体
degrees	セ氏温度　（℃）
Celsius	温度計のセ氏
start boiling	沸騰しはじめる
steam	蒸気

Unit 4-2 I did not do anything bad. ぼくの言い分

broke (break)	壊す
crash(ed)	（車を）ぶつける
believe	（人・ものを）信じる
indoors	屋内で
outdoors	屋外で
need	（~を）必要とする

Unit 4-3 I failed the test. テストに落ちた理由

fail(ed)	~を失敗する
aloud	声を出して
memorized	（~を）暗記する
sentence(s)	文章
chore(s) at home	（洗濯・掃除・片づけなど）家の雑用、家事
vacuum	（~を電気掃除機で）掃除する
empty	空（から）にする
trash can(s)	ゴミ箱
water the flowers	花に水やりをする
fold	折りたたむ
laundry	洗濯物
household chores	家事

feed	えさをやる
regularly	定期的に

Unit 5-1 A Post Card from Hawaii ハワイからの絵葉書

letting me (let me)	私に~させてくれて（私にさせる）
destination	目的地
leave	（場所を）出発する
arrive at~	~に到着する
ceremony	儀式、式典
the Changing of the Guard	衛兵交代
a one-day trip	日帰り旅行

Unit 5-2 I was the smallest tree in the forest. セコイアの木

grew (grow)	（木が）伸びた、生長した
forest	森

Unit 5-3 STORY: The Cow and the Frog イソップ物語 牛とカエル

once	かつて
hop(ped)	ぴょんぴょん跳ぶ
huge	巨大な
in the field	野外で、野原で
as ~ as	と同じくらい~
took (take) a deep breath	息を深く吸った
puff up	ふくらませる
became (become)	（~に）なった
finally	ついに、とうとう
pop(ped)	（音を立てて）破裂する
almost	ほとんど
therefore	したがって、その結果として

Unit 6-1 I want to stop by a convenience store to buy something to drink. コンビニに寄りたい

are (be) ready	用意が整って、準備ができて
stop by	立ち寄る
anything else	何か他のもの
borrow	~を借りる
reasonable	道理に合った
during	~の間ずっと
acceptable	受け入れられる
modify	部分的に手を加える
regularly	規則正しく、定期的に
proper temperature	適した温度
nutrient(s)	栄養素

Unit 6-2 I want you to leave me along. 僕のことはかまわないで

be nice to	優しく接する
the elderly	高齢者
while	~する間

Unit 6-3 I told you to do this. 言ったでしょ

aquarium	水族館
concert	演奏会、コンサート

Unit 7-1 Offering Good Advice アドバイスしてみよう

so that	~するために、~となるように
first of all	まず第一に
choose	~を選ぶ
information	情報、知識
had better not	~をしない方がよい
website(s)	ウェブサイト、ホームページ

Words and Phrases Glossary

script	原稿、スクリプト
prepare	(〜を)準備する、用意する
confident	自信をもって
audience	聴衆
stand straight	背筋を真っすぐ伸ばして立つ
keep your head up	頭を上げる
make eye contact with	(人)と目を合わせる、アイコンタクトをとる
friendly	友好的な、好意的な
take some medicine	薬を服用する
lost and found counter	拾得物預り所

Unit 7-2 I wish I could. できたら良いのに

come around	ぶらりとやってくる、立ち寄る
through	〜を通って
tunnel	トンネル
per second	毎秒
signature	サイン

Unit 7-3 Show and Tell お気に入りのおもちゃ

how to play	遊び方
all day long	1日じゅう
mean	意地の悪い
decide(d) to	(〜しようと)決める
the truth	真実
was shock(ed)	ショックを受けた

Unit 8-1 The man wearing a bright pink sweater どの人?

bright	(色が)鮮やかな
against the red light	赤信号を無視して
carry(ing)	運んでいる
shining	輝いている
appear(s)	現われる

Unit 8-2 A bird whose beak is yellow くちばしが黄色い鳥

beak	くちばし
dwarves (dwarf)	(おとぎ話に出てくる)小びと達
poisoned	毒入りの
made of glass	ガラス製の
carriage	四輪馬車
pheasant	キジ
save(d)	救う
castle	城
grew (grow) long	長く伸びる
told (tell) a lie	嘘をつく

Unit 8-3 The Peach Boy 桃太郎の簡単バージョンと詳しいバージョン

once upon a time	昔々
couple	夫婦
village	村
gather(ed)	かき集める
firewood	たきぎ
clothes	衣服
float(ing)	浮かんで(浮かぶ)
establish(ed)	創立する
shogunate	幕府
compose(d)	作曲する

Unit 9-1 Have you seen it yet? もう見た?

bridge	橋
not yet	まだ〜ない
decorate	飾る
get drinks	飲み物を準備する
never	一度も〜しない、決して〜ない

Unit 9-2 Have you seen a snake with legs? 見たことある?

wing(s)	翼
stripe(s)	ストライプ
shooting star	流れ星
stay(ed) up all night	徹夜する

Unit 9-3 The most beautiful sunset I have ever seen. 今までの中で一番!

sight	景色
cartoon	マンガ、アニメ映画
character	(マンガの)キャラクター

Unit 10-1 Where have you been? どこに行ってたの?

wait(ing) for	待っている
look(ing) for	探している
worry(ing) about	心配している
since	〜以来、〜の時からずっと
current	今の、現在の
already	もうすでに
still	まだ

Unit 10-2 Jack and the Beanstalk ジャックと豆の木

beanstalk	豆の木
hope	望み、希望
happiness	幸せ
exchange 〜 for...	〜を…と交換する
make〜 happy	〜を幸せにする
seed	種
burst into tears	泣き出す、泣きくずれる
puppy	子犬
tidy	(部屋が)きちんとした、整頓された

Unit 10-3 The language spoken there is English. そこで話されている言語は英語です

Let me try.	(ぼくに)試させて。
is (be) made from〜	〜(材料)で作られている
is (be) covered with〜	〜で覆われている
is (be) full of〜	〜で満ちている
are (be) cut by 〜	〜によって切られる
is (be) filled with〜	〜でいっぱいである
is (be) made of〜	〜でできている
is (be) pleased with〜	〜に喜んでいる
is (be) known to〜	〜で知られている
is (be) written in〜	〜で書かれている
igloo	イグルー《氷雪のかたまりで造るイヌイットの冬の住居》

supplement

Occupation Song

Lyrics by Mikiko Nakamoto
Composed by Charles A. Vilina
Arranged by Akiko Arai

※ We are doctors,
Nurses, teachers,
Police officers, shopkeepers,
Fire fighters and garbagemen, too,
Construction workers... "How do you do?"
Taxi and bus drivers in your town,
We always smile and never frown.

We are doctors, "Open your mouth."
We are teachers, "Listen to me."
We are nurses and drivers, too.
We are shopkeepers, "May I help you?"
Garbagemen take our trash away.
Police officers say, "Have a nice day."
Construction workers say, "Watch your step!"
We all work together.
(※repeat)

Open your mouth.   Listen to me.
May I help you?   Watch your step!
Have a nice day.

We all work together.

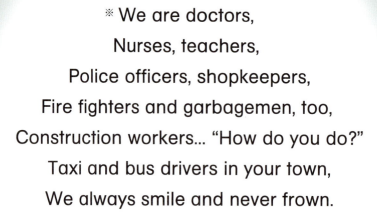

'Cause You're My Friend
Lyrics & Composed by Mikiko Nakamoto
Arranged by Larry Knapp

Oh, my dear friends,　ともだちよ
Please do not cry,　泣かないで
There's got to be something,
Though it may be little,
There's got to be something,
Something we can share.

Oh, my dear friends,　ともだちよ
Please do not cry,　泣かないで
何かがある　小さいけれど
きっと何か　分かち合えることが

あなたが何でも　あなたがだれでも
あなたがどこにいても　We love you so,
Whatever you are,
Whoever you are,
Wherever you are,　ともだちだから

Oh, my dear friends,　ともだちよ
Please look at me.　目をむけて
There's got to be something,
Though it may be little,
There's got to be something,
Something we can see.

The trees are there,
The stars are there,
The sun is there,
Waiting just for you.

The trees are there,
The stars are there,
The sun is there,　ともだちだから

Oh, my dear friends,　ともだちよ
Let's sing the song,　うたおうよ
La la la la la la la la la la la……

Photos by Yuzo Uda
Design by Toshikazu Mitsui

Learning World for TOMORROW ⑤ Syllabus

Unit	Topics	Grammar	Structures	Words & Phrases
1-1	大地の自己紹介 Me Myself	一般動詞1、2人称 / Be 動詞 Regular verbs 1st & 2nd person / Be verbs	■ I am good at ... I am afraid of ... I enjoy ... ■ I like ... I am ... I want ...	sports, playing a musical instrument, making friends, traveling in airplanes, being alone, blood, heights, thunderstorms, meeting new people, being on my own, very organized
1-2	美しい惑星―地球― The Beautiful Planet	現在進行形 / 三人称単数現在 Present Progressive / 3rd person singular	■ I am ...ing.	listening to music, sitting on the bench, standing under a big tree, talking to, the earth, the sun, cause, spin, axis, travel around, side, facing, heat, light, cool, dark, tilted
1-3	市長演説 The Mayor's Speech	Be 動詞 / 形容詞 Be verbs / Adjectives	■ There is ... / There are ... ■ The ... of our city is ...	restaurant, post office, police station, park, hospital, city hall, music hall, bakery, train station, elementary school, high school, fire station, supermarket, convenience store, amusement park, department store, humorous, quiet, unique, friendly, kind, popular, cool, smart, shy, sincere, adventurous, brave, athletic, tough, optimistic, energetic, young, diligent, cheerful, honest, ambitious, intelligent, noisy, proud, mayor, population
2-1	お友達の家へ Hello. Come in. Help yourself.	いろいろの定型表現 / 命令形 Set phrases & greetings / Imperative	■ Rinse the rice and drain the water several times.	have a seat, happy to be here, glad to hear that, see you again, keep in touch, say hello to, rinse, drain, press, beep, add, switch to, measure, scale, automatically, mode
2-2	おどろくべき動物たち Surprising Facts	真理・事実を伝える現在形 Present tense to tell the truth & facts	■ Butterflies taste with their feet? ■ Do you ...? Why ...? Can you ...? What ...?	dolphins, butterflies, crows, elephants, snails, squids, sea horses, lions, giraffes, pandas, ostriches, taste, remember, give birth, weigh, human, teeth, hearts, male
2-3	ぼくの過去・現在・未来 My Past, Present and Future	Be動詞 過去/現在/未来 Past, present and future tenses of be verbs	■ I was ... Now I am ... One day, I will be ...	a little egg, caterpillar, butterfly, leaves, tadpole, pond, frog, land, baby, astronaut, on a leaf, in the mud, in a pond, on the land, in my father's arms, at school, into space, on the table, on the TV
3-1	リサイクルを考える Recycling Garbage	未来形 Future: be going to	■ What are we going to do with them?	3Rs, reduce, reuse, recycle, separate, empty, flatten, donate, follow, cardboard, newspaper, glass, metal, plastic, bin, flyers, boxes, junk mail, packaging, policies, styrofoam trays, potato skins, fish bones, lids, containers, jars, scraps, trimmings
3-2	世界旅行プラン Starting off on a World Trip	未来形 Future: will	■ I will go to ... 　It will take me ... days to get there.	travel around the world, climb, Uluru, Ganges River, Turkey, cave, ibex, Algeria, camel, Sahara Desert, Colosseum, Venezuela, Angel Falls, itinerary, route
3-3	もう、十分な年齢です Asking Permission	原因・影響 / 程度を表す副詞 Why ...? Because ... / Enough, too, just right	■ Because you are too ... ■ I'm not too young. I'm old enough.	by yourself, by myself, anything, anything, get along with, be sure to, behave, just right, astronaut, selected, chosen
4-1	ぼくと妹の日課 My Routine Activities	一般動詞の現在形 / 三人称単数現在 Present tense regular verbs / 3rd person singular	■ I usually ... at ..., but Ibuki ... at ...	get up, make my/her bed, have breakfast, go to school, study English, do my/her homework, take a bath, watch TV, treat sick animals, write programs, collect news, write fiction stories, body, smell, taste, color, states, liquid, solid, gas, freezing, Celsius, boiling, steam
4-2	ぼくの言い分 I did not do anything bad.	一般動詞の過去形 / 不定詞 Regular verbs past tense / Infinitive	■ What did you do? ■ I tried to ...	clean the room, break/broke, cook dinner, wash the car, crash the car, indoors, outdoors
4-3	テストに落ちた理由 I failed the test.	過去形 Past tense	■ What did you do? 　I fed the fish.	aloud, memorize, household chores, vacuum the living room, empty the trash cans, water the flowers, fold the laundry
5-1	ハワイからの絵葉書 A postcard from Hawaii	一般動詞の過去形/未来形(be going to) Past and future tenses (be going to)	■ He took me to the beach yesterday. ■ We're going to hike to the top of the mountain.	leave/left, stay/stayed, see/saw, go/went, arrive/arrived, visit/visited, take/took, have/had, destination, period, ceremony, one-day trip
5-2	セコイアの木 I was the smallest tree.	比較級 / 最上級 Comparatives / Superlatives	■ Are you taller than Kelly? ■ I am taller. I am the tallest.	little, short/shorter (than)/the shortest, tall/taller (than)/the tallest, big/bigger (than)/the biggest, old/older (than)/the oldest, spring, summer, fall, winter, forest
5-3	イソップ物語 牛とカエル STORY:The Cow and the Frog	比較級 Comparison: as ... as	■ A frog is as big as a ball.	as big as, huge, field, mountain, puff up, much, even deeper, even more, boom, almost, therefore, country, China, the USA, Russia, Canada, England, Germany

Unit	Title	Grammar Point	Example Sentences	Vocabulary
6-1	コンビニに寄りたい I want to stop by a convenience store to buy something to drink.	不定詞3用法 Infinitives	■ I think it's reasonable to clean our classroom ourselves.	to stop by, something, reasonable, school uniform, ourselves, acceptable, dye, make-up, modify, regularly, on the way back, proper temperature, nutrients, leaves, roots
6-2	僕のことはかまわないで I want you to leave me alone.	不定詞 Infinitives (want you to ...)	■ I don't want anyone to read my diary.	leave me alone, offer my seat to the elderly, study at university, while I am out, read my diary
6-3	言ったでしょ I told you to do this.	疑問詞+不定詞 Question words + infinitives	■ I don't know what to do. ■ Do you know how to get there?	tell me everything, what to do, where to go, when to go, how to go, anything, go surfing, go skiing, go on a picnic, museum, aquarium, concert hall, shopping mall
7-1	アドバイスしてみよう Offering Good Advice	助動詞 Modal auxiliaries: should, have to, have got to, must	■ What should I do? ■ If I were you, I would ...	should, have to, have got to, had better, must, if I were you, advice, choose, topic, web sites, some, all, script, prepare, practice, confident, in front of, mirror, audience, memorize, stand straight, make eye contact, look friendly, take some medicine, lost and found, counter, improve
7-2	できたら良いのに I wish I could.	If節 直接法 / 仮定法 If: first and second conditionals	■ If you are free, please come around. ■ If I were free, I'd be happy to come over.	come around, get lost, come over, afraid I can't, I wish I could, length, police box, in my pocket, donate, offer my seat, do nothing, signature, shake hands
7-3	お気に入りのおもちゃ Show and Tell	SVOO Subject-Verb-Object-Object	■ I'll show you a book.	boing, rodeo, donkey, do something mean, tell her the truth, shocked, still, always, home economics
8-1	どの人? The man wearing a bright pink sweater.	現在分詞の形容詞用法 Adjectives: participle phrases	■ The dog running with a boy ■ The star shining brightly	cross the street, against the red light, chase, Venus, star, shining brightly, in the west, in the east, before, after, sunset, sunrise, evening star, morning star
8-2	くちばしが黄色い鳥 A bird whose beak is yellow.	現在分詞 / 関係代名詞 Present participles / Relative pronouns	■ A bird whose beak is yellow.	which, who, whose, where, in the tree, over there, beak, naughty, dwarf/dwarves, poisoned, made of, made from, be born, pheasant, save, under the sea, on the moon, tell a lie
8-3	桃太郎の簡単バージョンと詳しいバージョン STORY: The Peach Boy	現在分詞 / 関係代名詞 Present participles / Relative pronouns	■ This is the house where I live.	which, who, where, in the tree, over there, once upon a time, old couple, old man, old lady, gather firewood, be floating down the stream, collect something, go abroad, officially, establish, compose, symphony
9-1	もう見た? Have you seen it yet?	現在完了 (完了) Present perfect (completed action)	■ Have you ... yet? Yes, I have. / No, I haven't. I have finished cooking.	see/saw/seen, go/went/gone, eat/ate/eaten, take/took/taken, do/did/done, clean/cleaned/cleaned, get/got/got, set/set/set, decorate/decorated/decorated, finish/finished/finished, already, yet
9-2	見たことある? Have you ever seen a snake with legs?	現在完了 (経験) Present perfect (experience)	■ Have you ever ...? I have never seen a ghost.	ever, never, only, wings, without, ghost, you're kidding, I can't believe it, meet a famous person, be on TV, ride a horse or a pony, shooting star, stay up all night, exciting thing
9-3	今までの中で一番！ The most beautiful sunset I have ever seen.	現在完了 Present perfect: the most ... I have ever ...	■ You are the nicest teacher I have ever met.	let me show you, amazing, shopping center, pancakes, thoughtful, wonderful
10-1	どこに行ってたの? Where have you been?	現在完了進行形 Present perfect continuous	■ I have been studying English for seven years since I was five.	wait for, look for, worry about, since, for, current home, be good friends with, how long, when
10-2	ジャックと豆の木 STORY: Jack and the Beanstalk	SVOC Subject-Verb-Object-Complement	■ I named it Tarra. ■ What makes you happy? I have finished cooking.	tiny, seed, hope, happiness, exchange, on the way, burst into tears, believe, something, just as, puppy, keep my room, tidy
10-3	そこで話されている言語は英語です The language spoken there is English.	受動態 Passive voice	■ This wine is made by my father.	hill, be covered with, vines, full of, barrel, filled with, made of, made from, made by, be pleased with, speak/spoken, take/taken, write/written, give/given, know/known, draw/drawn, eat/eaten, make/made, tell/told, bring/brought, keep/kept, Russian, Greek, Polish, Chinese, Thai, Korean, paper, mud, stones, bricks, ice, wood, straw, sand, structure, house, church, temple, next

PROGRESS REPORT

My name is _____

Reciting

4	24	44
6	26	46
8	28	48
10	30	50
12	32	52
14	34	54
16	36	56
18	38	58
20	40	60
22	42	62

Writing

4	24	44
6	26	46
8	28	48
10	30	50
12	32	52
14	34	54
16	36	56
18	38	58
20	40	60
22	42	62

Challenge Chart

Date	1	2	3	4	5	6	7	8	9	10	11	12	Total

Date	1	2	3	4	5	6	7	8	9	10	11	12	Total

先生の質問に答えて色をぬりましょう。

Students color in one happy face at a time on answering each of the teacher's questions during warm up/review time.

Certificate of Achievement

Awarded to _____

this _____ day of _____ ,

for your great effort in

Learning World 5 for TOMORROW

Signed _____